モギケンの英語シャワーBOX 実践版
茂木健一郎

朝日出版社

Contents

CDブックの構成と使い方 —————————————————— 4

15. 老人と海
The Old Man and the Sea —————————————————— 8

16. 風と共に去りぬ
Gone with the Wind —————————————————— 16

17. グレート・ギャツビー
The Great Gatsby —————————————————— 30

18. ジェーン・エア
Jane Eyre —————————————————— 42

19. 嵐が丘
Wuthering Heights —————————————————— 54

20. 高慢と偏見
Pride and Prejudice —————————————————— 66

21. ガーデン・パーティー
The Garden Party —————————————————— 80

22. ボーディング・ハウス
The Boarding House —————————————————— 92

23. アッシャー家の崩壊
The Fall of the House of Usher —————————————————— 100

Column
大人のための壮大なファンタジー、『指輪物語』の魅力 —————————————————— 40
古典文学の天才、シェイクスピアの戯曲に挑戦 —————————————————— 78
オスカー・ワイルドが描いた、拒絶された人間にこそある「真実」 —————————————————— 108

CDブックの構成と使い方

3STEPで段階的にレベルアップ

このCDブックは、次の3つのステップで段階的にレベルアップできるように構成してあります。

STEP1 HOP

ピーターラビット・シリーズや『星の王子さま』など、絵本や子供向けの作品から、大人でも十分に楽しめる『赤毛のアン』といった作品が収録されています。子供向けであっても一口に簡単とは言えませんが、ネイティブが子供の頃に読んできた作品に触れることで、まずは英語シャワーに慣れてください。

STEP2 STEP

大人向けの英語から、比較的読みやすいものをセレクトしました。僕が学生時代にテキストとして使った『Background to Britain』やオバマ大統領の演説、オー・ヘンリーの短編などが収録されています。中学英語を勉強した人であれば、それほど難しくない作品ばかりだと思います。英語シャワーの「流れ」を感じられるように読んでみてください。

STEP3 JUMP

『老人と海』や『風と共に去りぬ』など、ネイティブの大人が読む小説なので、少々手強いかもしれませんが、どれも僕が読んで感動した名作ばかりです。和訳で読んだことのある作品からチャレンジすれば、多少わからないところがあっても、英語の"美味しさ"を味わえるのではないかと思います。

作品の難易度

それぞれの作品の最初のページに、難易度を星のマークで示してあります。星の数が多いほど、英語のレベルが高くなりますが、必ずしも **STEP1** が星一つとは限りません。読むときの目安にしてください。

- 難易度 ★☆☆　比較的簡単
- 難易度 ★★☆　それほど難しくない
- 難易度 ★★★　チャレンジしがいがあり

CDブックの構成と使い方

CDブックの使い方

　作品の「あらすじ」を読んだ後、鑑賞のヒントとなる日本語のエッセイを読みながら、対応する部分の Scene の原文にチャレンジしてください。

　まず最初は、赤い下敷きを重ねて、わからない単語があっても流れを止めずに、最後まで読んでください。次に、本を見ながら朗読CDを聞いた後、今度は自分で声に出して何度か読んでみます。そして最後に下敷きを取り、知りたい単語をチェックします。

❶ あらすじをチェックする
❷ エッセイを読みながら、原文にチャレンジする
❸ 朗読CDを聞く
❹ 声に出して読む
❺ わからない単語を確認する

15. The Old Man and the Sea

16. Gone with the Wind

17. The Great Gatsby

18. Jane Eyre

19. Wuthering Heights

20. Pride and Prejudice

21. The Garden Party

22. The Boarding House

23. The Fall of the House of Usher

15 老人と海

「ハードボイルド・スタイル」で知られる
ダイヤモンドの原石のような文章

> **原題** The Old Man and the Sea
> **著者** Ernest Hemingway
> **発表** 1952年
>
> あらすじ：長く不漁が続く老人は、ある日一人で漁に出る。太陽が真上にさしかかった頃、老人の網に獲物がかかる。獲物が大物であることを感じとった老人は、慎重に網を引き、懸命にたぐり寄せようとする。しかし魚も負けてはおらず、老人の舟を沖へ引っ張っていく。ここから、老人と魚の死闘が始まる。

孤独な男の人生との戦い

　言わずと知れたアメリカの作家アーネスト・ヘミングウェイ（Ernest Hemingway）の中編小説です。孤独な老人が一人海に漕ぎ出し、巨大な魚を釣り上げるために延々と格闘し続ける。その一連の話を淡々と描いた作品です。

　物語は巨大な獲物との四日間にわたる死闘を描いたもの。釣り上げた魚は結局サメに喰われてしまうため、老人の決死の戦いは、

徒労に終わってしまいます。しかし、ここには「孤独の魂としての人間が、いかにして人生に立ち向かうか」というテーマの、一つのアレゴリー（寓話）が描かれています。それは作者自身の人生をも想起させるものです。

人間が巨大な相手と戦うという神話的なストーリーは、ハーマン・メルヴィル（Herman Melville）の『白鯨』（Moby-Dick）に通じるものがあります。

巨大な魚との対決

主人公の老人は、ここのところずっと漁で獲物を獲れずに終わっています。縁起かつぎをする漁師仲間たちの間では、このように長い間魚を獲れない漁師はツキに見放されていると噂されます。それまで漁を手伝ってくれていた心優しい少年は、あれこれと老人を気遣ってくれますが、少年にも自分と家族の生活があります。いつまでも魚が獲れない老人と一緒にいることはできません。老人もそれを十分にわかっているので、たった一人で大海原へと漕ぎ出したのでした。

夜明け前の暗いうちに小舟を出した老人は、太陽が高く昇るころに巨大な獲物がかかっている感触を得ます。ところが何時間たっても、獲物の魚は悠々と老人の小舟を曳きながら、沖へ向かっ

て泳ぐのをやめません。老人は魚の姿を見ることもできないまま、獲物のかかった綱を離さないようにして長い夜を過ごすことになります。 `Scene1` はその翌日、老人がようやく巨大な魚と対面する場面です。

　相手の姿を見てからというもの老人は、紫色の胸びれを翼のようにひろげ、大きな尾をぴんと立てて黒々とした水を切って泳ぐ魚の姿を、まざまざと思い描くことができました。しかし、その後もなかなか水面に上がってこようとしない魚との長い根くらべが始まります。老人は意識が朦朧とする中、ときどき魚に話しかけたり独り言をつぶやいたりするのでした。 `Scene2`

短いセンテンスを重ねる、筋肉質な文体
　老人のせりふには、人間の驕りや愚かさを非難するヘミングウェイの自然観がよく現れています。そして最後の対決の場面からは、老人の魚に対する深い愛情を読みとることができます。 `Scene3` `Scene4`

　ヘミングウェイの文体は決して単純なものではありませんが、短いセンテンスを積み重ねていく筋肉質な文体は、ダイヤモンドの原石を思わせるような輝きを放っています。

The Old Man and the Sea
老人と海

Scene1

The line rose slowly and steadily and then the surface of the ocean bulged ahead of the boat and the fish came out. He came out unendingly and water poured from his sides. He was bright in the sun and his head and back were dark purple and in the sun the stripes on his sides showed wide and a light lavender. His sword was as long as a baseball bat and tapered like a rapier and he rose his full length from the water and then re-entered it, smoothly, like a diver and the old man saw the great scythe-blade of his tail go under and the line commenced to race out.

"He is two feet longer than the skiff," the old man said. The line was going out fast but steadily and the fish was not panicked. The old man was trying with both hands to keep the line just inside of breaking strength. He knew that if he could not slow the fish with a steady pressure the fish could take out all the line and break it.

Scene2

"How do you feel, fish?" he asked aloud. "I feel good and my left hand is better and I have food for a night and a day. Pull the boat, fish."

He did not truly feel good because the pain from the cord across his back had almost passed pain and gone into a dullness that he mistrusted. But I have had worse things than that, he thought. My hand is only cut a little and the cramp is gone from the other. My legs are all right. Also now I have gained on him in the question of sustenance.

Scene3

"The fish is my friend too," he said aloud. "I have never seen or heard of such a fish. But I must kill him. I am glad we do not have to try to kill the stars."

Imagine if each day a man must try to kill the moon, he thought. The moon runs away. But imagine if a man each day should have to try to kill the sun? We were born lucky, he thought.

Then he was sorry for the great fish that had nothing to eat and his determination to kill him never relaxed in his sorrow for him. How many people will he feed, he thought. But are they worthy to eat him? No, of course not. There is no one worthy of eating him from the manner of his behaviour and his great dignity.

I do not understand these things, he thought. But it is good that we do not have to try to kill the sun or the moon or the stars. It is enough to live on the sea and kill our true brothers.

##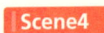

The fish was coming in on his circle now calm and beautiful-looking and only his great tail moving. The old man pulled on him all that he could to bring him closer. For just a moment the fish turned a little on his side. Then he straightened himself and began another circle.

"I moved him," the old man said. "I moved him then."

He felt faint again now but he held on the great fish all the strain that he could. I moved him, he thought. Maybe this time I can get him over. Pull, hands, he thought. Hold up, legs. Last for me, head. Last for me. You never went. This time I'll pull him over. But when he put all of his effort on, starting it well out before the fish came alongside and pulling with all his strength, the fish pulled part way over and then righted himself and swam away.

"Fish," the old man said. "Fish, you are going to have to die anyway. Do you have to kill me too?"

That way nothing is accomplished, he thought. His mouth was too dry to speak but he could not reach for the water now. I must get him alongside this time, he thought. I am not good for many more turns. Yes you are, he told himself. You're good for ever.

On the next turn, he nearly had him. But again the fish righted himself and swam slowly away.

You are killing me, fish, the old man thought. But you have a right to. Never have I seen a greater, or more beautiful, or a calmer or more noble thing than you, brother. Come on and kill me. I do not care who kills who.

16 風と共に去りぬ

難易度 ★★☆

大学への通学電車で読みふけった
エンターテインメント小説の最高峰

> 原題 Gone with the Wind
> 著者 Margaret Munnerlyn Mitchell
> 発表 1936年
>
> あらすじ：舞台は南北戦争のアメリカ南部。美しく誇り高いスカーレットが恋するアシュレーは、従姉妹のメラニーと婚約してしまう。失意のスカーレットの前に無頼漢的なレット・バトラーが現れ、彼女に求愛する。スカーレットはアシュレーへの想いを捨てきれずにいるが、しだいにレットに惹かれていく。

グイグイと引き込まれる物語の面白さ

　短編小説の良さはすぐに読み終わることですが、長編小説には長編小説なりの良さがあります。何より、読み終わった時の達成感もひとしおです。

　『風と共に去りぬ』(Gone with the Wind) を、僕は大学一年生の頃に、通学する銀座線の行き帰りで読みましたが、疲れ果てて "死んだ" 記憶があります。必死になって読み進めてもなかなか終わ

らない。しかし、エンターテインメント小説の良いところは、それでもグイグイと物語に引き込まれて読み進めていけるところです。

　アメリカの女性作家、マーガレット・ミッチェル（Margaret Mitchell）によって書かれたこの作品は、アメリカ南北戦争を背景に、美しく気位の高い主人公スカーレット・オハラの半生を壮大に描いた小説です。

男が惚れる無頼漢、レット・バトラー

　南部の裕福な農園主の娘で美貌の持ち主のスカーレットは、同じく裕福な上流階級でハンサムなアシュレーに恋をしています。しかし彼は従姉妹のメラニーと婚約しており、どんなにスカーレットが望んでも彼女の愛を拒みます。そこに魅力的ではあるものの少々無頼漢的なレット・バトラーが現れ、スカーレットに求愛するのです。

　物語はスカーレットの恋愛の行方を軸に、彼ら上流階級がこれまで何の疑いも持ってこなかった社会──白人による黒人の奴隷支配──が、南北戦争を境に崩壊していくさまを描いています。

　この小説が絶対的に面白いのは、キャラクター造形が豊かだからです。女性は圧倒的に主人公のスカーレットに感情移入をするようですが、男性としてはメラニーの方に好意を抱く。そして、何

よりレット・バトラーという人物が面白い。とことんニヒルで、周囲の人間が信じる価値などほとんど馬鹿にしているのに、いざ戦争が始まったら、負けを知りながら戦地に赴く。そこが男ながらに「おぉ！」と惚れそうになるわけです。

　Scene1 は、北軍が攻め入り戦地と化したアトランタを後に、スカーレットが故郷タラに逃れる場面です。レットは突然、彼女を残して戦場に向かうと言う。それを聞いたスカーレットは不安と恐怖で途方に暮れ、彼に詰め寄ります。 Scene2

　レット・バトラーはそれまでスカーレットに「好きだが、愛してはいない」とクールに言い放ってきたのですが、ここで初めて自分が彼女を愛していることを告白するのです。 Scene3

　熱いくちづけに一時理性を失いうっとりする彼女でしたが、すぐに現実を思い出し、われに返ります。 Scene4

辞書を使わずに、意味を推察する

　この小説のもう一つの魅力は、会話が「生きている」ところです。映画でも印象的な台詞が多く出てきますが、原作の小説の会話が生き生きとしているからこそ、そのまま台本としても活きてくるのでしょう。

　会話と言えば、スカーレットがよく口にする口癖があります。そ

れは "Great balls of fire!" と、"fiddle dee-dee" というものです。相手が何かを言ったときに、それを封じるためのフレーズとして使っており、「なんてこと！」というような意味だと理解していました。

ちなみに、原書を読むときに「辞書は使わない」主義の僕は、今回初めてこの言葉を辞書で調べてみました。"fiddle dee-dee" は「ナンセンス」という意味だそうです。

原書を読む場合、僕たち日本人がやってしまいがちな「一語一句を頭の中で日本語に訳す」ことを、まずは意識的にやめてみるといいと思います。わからない単語が出てきても、前後の文脈から大体の意味と使い方を察してみるのです。

あまりに有名なラストシーン

最後の Scene5 は、映画でも大変印象的だったラストシーンです。常に傍にいて支えあってきた友人メラニーを亡くし、最愛のレットも彼女の元から去って行った。悲しみに打ちひしがれるスカーレットでしたが、再び故郷のタラに戻り、すべてを一からやり直すことを決心します。

やはり、見事です。みなさんもぜひ一度、エンターテインメント小説の最高峰、『風と共に去りぬ』の世界に浸ってみてください。

Gone with the Wind

風と共に去りぬ

Scene1 CD3 5

"Good. Maybe you can get past Rough and Ready
通過する　ラフ・アンド・レディ（場所）
all right. General Steve Lee was there during the
うまく　将軍
afternoon covering the retreat. Maybe the Yankees
援護しながら　退却　北軍兵
aren't there yet. Maybe you can get through there, if
通過する
Steve Lee's men don't pick up your horse."
取り上げる

"I—*I* can get through?"

"Yes, *you*." His voice was rough.
荒っぽい

"But Rhett—You—Aren't you going to take us?"

"No. I'm leaving you here."

She looked around wildly, at the livid sky behind
辺りを見回す　鉛色の
them, at the dark trees on either hand hemming them
彼らを取り囲んでいる
in like a prison wall, at the frightened figures in the
牢獄　おびえた　人々
back of the wagon—and finally at him. Had she gone
奥に　荷馬車　最後に
crazy? Was she not hearing right?
気が狂う

He was grinning now. She could just see his white teeth in the faint light and the old mockery was back in his eyes.

"Leaving us? Where—where are you going?"

"I am going, dear girl, with the army."

She sighed with relief and irritation. Why did he joke at this time of all times? Rhett in the army! After all he'd said about stupid fools who were enticed into losing their lives by a roll of drums and brave words from orators—fools who killed themselves that wise men might make money!

"Oh, I could choke you for scaring me so! Let's get on."

"I'm not joking, my dear. And I am hurt, Scarlett, that you do not take my gallant sacrifice with better spirit. Where is your patriotism, your love for Our Glorious Cause? Now is your chance to tell me to return with my shield or on it. But, talk fast, for I want time to make a brave speech before departing for the wars."

His drawling voice jibed in her ears. He was jeering at her and, somehow, she knew he was jeering at himself too. What was he talking about? Patriotism, shields, brave speeches? It wasn't possible that he meant what he was saying.

Scene2

"Rhett, you are joking!"

She grabbed his arm and felt her tears of fright splash down on her wrist. He raised her hand and kissed it airily.

"Selfish to the end, aren't you, my dear? Thinking only of your own precious hide and not of the gallant Confederacy. Think how our troops will be heartened by my eleventh-hour appearance." There was a malicious tenderness in his voice.

"Oh, Rhett," she wailed, "how can you do this to me? Why are you leaving me?"

"Why?" he laughed jauntily. "Because, perhaps, of the betraying sentimentality that lurks in all of us Southerners. Perhaps—perhaps because I am ashamed. Who knows?"

"Ashamed? You should die of shame. To desert us here, alone, helpless—"

"Dear Scarlett! You aren't helpless. Anyone as selfish and determined as you are is never helpless. God help the Yankees if they should get you."

"I'm not asking you to understand or forgive. I don't give a damn whether you do either, for I shall never understand or forgive myself for this idiocy. I am annoyed at myself to find that so much quixoticism still lingers in me. But our fair Southland needs every man. Didn't our brave Governor Brown say just that? No matter. I'm off to the wars." He laughed suddenly, a ringing, free laugh that startled the echoes in the dark woods.

"'I could not love thee, Dear, so much, loved I not Honour more.' That's a pat speech, isn't it? Certainly better than anything I can think up myself, at the present moment. For I do love you, Scarlett, in spite of what I said that night on the porch last month."

His drawl was caressing and his hands slid up her bare arms, warm strong hands. "I love you, Scarlett, because we are so much alike, renegades, both of us, dear, and selfish rascals. Neither of us cares a rap if the whole world goes to pot, so long as we are safe and comfortable."

His voice went on in the darkness and she heard words, but they made no sense to her. Her mind was tiredly trying to take in the harsh truth that he was leaving her here to face the Yankees alone. Her mind said: "He's leaving me. He's leaving me." But no emotion stirred.

Then his arms went around her waist and shoulders and she felt the hard muscles of his thighs against her body and the buttons of his coat pressing into her breast. A warm tide of feeling, bewildering, frightening, swept over her, carrying out of her mind the time and place and circumstances. She felt as limp as a rag doll, warm, weak and helpless, and his supporting arms were so pleasant.

"You don't want to change your mind about what I said last month? There's nothing like danger and death to give an added fillip. Be patriotic, Scarlett. Think how you would be sending a soldier to his death with beautiful memories."

He was kissing her now and his mustache tickled her mouth, kissing her with slow, hot lips that were as leisurely as though he had the whole night before him. Charles had never kissed her like this. Never had the kisses of the Tarleton and Calvert boys made her go hot and cold and shaky like this. He bent her body backward and his lips traveled down her throat to where the cameo fastened her basque.

"Sweet," he whispered. "Sweet."

Scene4

Into her swaying, darkened mind, cold sanity came back with a rush and she remembered what she had forgotten for the moment—that she was frightened too, and Rhett was leaving her, leaving her, the damned cad. And on top of it all, he had the consummate gall to stand here in the road and insult her with his infamous proposals. Rage and hate flowed into her and stiffened her spine and with one wrench she tore herself loose from his arms.

"Oh, you cad!" she cried and her mind leaped about, trying to think of worse things to call him, things she had heard Gerald call Mr. Lincoln, the MacIntoshes and balky mules, but the words would not come. "You low-down, cowardly, nasty, stinking thing!" And because she could not think of anything crushing enough, she drew back her arm and slapped him across the mouth with all the force she had left. He took a step backward, his hand going to his face.

"Ah," he said quietly and for a moment they stood facing each other in the darkness. Scarlett could hear his heavy breathing, and her own breath came in gasps as if she had been running hard.

"They were right! Everybody was right! You aren't a gentleman!"

"My dear girl," he said, "how inadequate."

She knew he was laughing and the thought goaded her.

"Go on! Go on now! I want you to hurry. I don't want to ever see you again. I hope a cannon ball lands right on you. I hope it blows you to a million pieces. I—"

"Never mind the rest. I follow your general idea. When I'm dead on the altar of my country, I hope your conscience hurts you."

She heard him laugh as he turned away and walked back toward the wagon.

Scene5

With the spirit of her people who would not know defeat, even when it stared them in the face, she raised her chin. She could get Rhett back. She knew she could. There had never been a man she couldn't get, once she set her mind upon him.

"I'll think of it all tomorrow, at Tara. I can stand it then. Tomorrow, I'll think of some way to get him back. After all, tomorrow is another day."

17 グレート・ギャツビー

難易度 ★★★

1920年代アメリカの富の象徴、華麗なるギャツビー

> 原題　The Great Gatsby
> 著者　Francis Scott Fitzgerald
> 発表　1925年
>
> あらすじ：証券会社に勤めるニック・キャラウェイは、ニューヨーク郊外のロング・アイランドにある高級住宅地へと引っ越してくる。隣の大邸宅では夜ごと豪華なパーティーが開かれており、その屋敷の主はジェイ・ギャツビーという謎の多い人物であることを知る。ある日、ニックはギャツビーのパーティーに招かれ、やがてギャツビーが長い間胸に秘めていたある野望を知ることになる。

世界大恐慌前夜のアメリカが舞台

アメリカの作家スコット・フィッツジェラルド（Francis Scott Fitzgerald）による中編小説。第一次世界大戦と第二次世界大戦にはさまれた過渡期的時代、世界大恐慌前夜のアメリカの豊かさと退廃を背景に、一人の男の夢と挫折を描いた作品です。

物語はニック・キャラウェイという青年の語りで紡がれていき

ます。ニックはニューヨークの証券会社に職を得たため、会社の通勤圏内にあるベッドタウンに引っ越してきます。彼が借りた家はごく普通の借家でしたが、その隣には豪奢な大邸宅が立っていました。大理石のプールに広大な芝生の庭、蔦の絡まる豪華な屋敷では、夜な夜な豪勢なパーティーが開かれ、大勢の客人が乱痴気騒ぎを繰り広げていました。

その屋敷の主人の名は、ジェイ・ギャツビー。夜ごとパーティーが催されるにもかかわらず、彼がどのような身分で、なぜそれほど財力があるのか、誰も正確な情報を知らないという謎に包まれた人物でした。

ギャツビーの秘密

ニックはギャツビー邸と入り江をはさんで立つ、もう一つの邸宅に住むトム・ビュキャナンのかつての学友であり、その妻デイジーとは、はとこの関係にあります。

ある夜、ビュキャナン家でのひとときを過ごして帰宅した彼は、星空の下、一人の男が芝生の上に佇(たたず)んでいるのを目にします。ギャツビーと思しきその男は、ちょうど入り江の向こうのビュキャナン邸の方角を向き、その先に瞬く小さな光に向かって手を差し伸べていたのでした。 Scene1

その場は言葉を交わすことなくすれ違ってしまったニックでしたが、ある日、正式に招かれたパーティーの席で、初めてギャツビー氏と顔を合わせます。若く、礼儀正しいギャツビーは、彼に親しみと不思議な印象を残します。以来、ニックに親しげに近づいてくるギャツビーは、ある秘密を抱えていました。

青春の"その後"を描いた作品

　サリンジャーの『ライ麦畑でつかまえて』が、永遠の青春小説だとすれば、この『グレート・ギャツビー』は青春の"その後"を描いた作品です。若いときのほとばしるような情熱、理由なき倦怠、未来への漠然とした不安……。そうしたものを抱えて青春時代を駆け抜けた青年たちは、徐々に現実を受け入れ、かつて夢見た理想と今ある現実の姿のギャップに悩みながらも、日常の生活を営むようになります。

　"Vulnerability"――これがこの小説の、あるいは多くのアメリカ文学を貫く一つのテーマではないでしょうか。つまり、「傷つきやすさ」とでも呼べるようなものです。

　この小説の冒頭の文章にも、vulnerable という単語が登場します。 Scene2

　みずみずしい若さや輝かしい富は、いつかは衰えて失われてい

きます。青春時代に持っていたものが、いつか消え去ってしまうことに対する潜在的な恐怖心。それがアメリカ文学の根底に常に流れているメッセージなのかもしれません。

そして、その富と若さを兼ね添えた人物こそが、グレート・ギャツビーでした。彼の莫大な富はどこからきているのか、なぜこの土地に邸宅を構え、夜ごとのパーティーを開いているのか、どうしてニックに関心を持ち、近づこうとしているのか……。物語がすすむにつれて、その謎が次第に明らかになっていきます。

「英語の本質」を体現した文体

次のシーンは、ニックと女友達のジョーダン・ベイカーが会話をする場面です。ジョーダンは実はかつて一度だけ、もう何年も前にギャツビーと顔を合わせたことがありました。そしてギャツビーは彼女を通じて、ニックにある頼み事をしてきたのでした。それは、彼のはとこのデイジー・ビュキャナンに関することでした。

Scene3

物語はこうしてギャツビーの過去へ、彼が抱き続けたある想いへとさかのぼり、急展開を遂げていきます。

この作品の文体は、非常に短く理解しやすいリズムで描かれて

います。持って回ったくどい冗長さを何より嫌う英語の本質を、見事に体現している文体と言えます。村上春樹氏など、アメリカ国内外を問わず、多くの作家にインスピレーションを与え続けてきたこの小説は、間違いなく現代を代表する作品の一つでしょう。

The Great Gatsby

グレート・ギャツビー

Already it was deep summer on roadhouse roofs and in front of wayside garages, where new red petrol-pumps sat out in pools of light, and when I reached my estate at West Egg I ran the car under its shed and sat for a while on an abandoned grass roller in the yard. The wind had blown off, leaving a loud, bright night, with wings beating in the trees and a persistent organ sound as the full bellows of the earth blew the frogs full of life. The silhouette of a moving cat wavered across the moonlight, and, turning my head to watch it, I saw that I was not alone—fifty feet away a figure had emerged from the shadow of my neighbor's mansion and was standing with his hands in his pockets regarding the silver pepper of the stars.

Something in his leisurely movements and the secure position of his feet upon the lawn suggested that it was Mr. Gatsby himself, come out to determine what share was his of our local heavens.

I decided to call to him. Miss Baker had mentioned him at dinner, and that would do for an introduction. But I didn't call to him, for he gave a sudden intimation that he was content to be alone—he stretched out his arms toward the dark water in a curious way, and, far as I was from him, I could have sworn he was trembling. Involuntarily I glanced seaward—and distinguished nothing except a single green light, minute and far away, that might have been the end of a dock. When I looked once more for Gatsby he had vanished, and I was alone again in the unquiet darkness.

Scene2

In my younger and more vulnerable years my father gave me some advice that I've been turning over in my mind ever since.

"Whenever you feel like criticizing anyone," he told me, "just remember that all the people in this world haven't had the advantages that you've had."

He didn't say any more, but we've always been unusually communicative in a reserved way, and I understood that he meant a great deal more than that.

Scene3

"It was a strange coincidence," I said.

"But it wasn't a coincidence at all."

"Why not?"

"Gatsby bought that house so that Daisy would be

just across the bay."

Then it had not been merely the stars to which he had aspired on that June night. He came alive to me, delivered suddenly from the womb of his purposeless splendour.

"He wants to know," continued Jordan, "if you'll invite Daisy to your house some afternoon and then let him come over."

The modesty of the demand shook me. He had waited five years and bought a mansion where he dispensed starlight to casual moths—so that he could "come over" some afternoon to a stranger's garden.

"Did I have to know all this before he could ask such a little thing?"

"He's afraid, he's waited so long. He thought you might be offended. You see, he's regular tough underneath it all."

Something worried me.

"Why didn't he ask you to arrange a meeting?"

"He wants her to see his house," she explained. "And your house is right next door."

"Oh!"

"I think he half expected her to wander into one of his parties, some night," went on Jordan, "but she never did. Then he began asking people casually if they knew her, and I was the first one he found. It was that night he sent for me at his dance, and you should have heard the elaborate way he worked up to it. Of course, I immediately suggested a luncheon in New York—and I thought he'd go mad:

" 'I don't want to do anything out of the way!' he kept saying. 'I want to see her right next door.'…"

Column
大人のための壮大なファンタジー、『指輪物語』の魅力

深い物語性と、圧倒的な面白さ

　僕が『指輪物語』(The Lord of the Rings) を読んだのは高校生のときです。映画化でも話題となったこの作品の原作は1954〜55年に発表され、その後長期的なブームとなりました。その当時、流行はまだ続いており、世界のベストセラーとして新聞に紹介されていたのがきっかけで興味を持ち、まずは瀬田貞二さんの訳で読み、その後原書に挑戦しました。

　『指輪物語』は、ホビット、エルフ、ドワーフ、人間、魔法使いなどさまざまな種族が住む架空世界を舞台に、すべてを統べることのできる一つの指輪をめぐる冒険と戦争を描いた物語です。

　指輪を持った者は不老不死の力を与えられ、権力を得ることもできます。しかし、指輪の魔性によって邪悪なものが指輪を持つ者の心を蝕んでいく──。『指輪物語』の心理描写は翳りが多く、複雑な心情と哀切さを感じさせてくれる、非常に奥深いファンタジー作品

です。

　この物語は、ホビットやエルフといった北欧神話やケルト神話から生まれたさまざまな種族の存在が魅力の一つです。作者のトールキン（J. R. R. Tolkien）が作り上げた架空の世界はとても詳細で、登場人物の系図や「ルーン文字」、独自の「エルフ語」の発明や歴史といったさまざまな文化的背景を含む完全な世界を構築しています。そのため物語性は深くかつ圧倒的に面白く、高校生だった僕はたちまちその世界の虜となりました。

　例えば、ルーン文字をまねして秘密の日記を書いたり、第１部『旅の仲間』に出てくる「モリアの坑道」に入るためのアーチ形にエルフ文字を組み合わせた扉を色紙で作り、部屋に飾ったりしていました。そのころは、定期テストが終わったら『指輪物語』の続きを読むのが楽しみ、という感じでした。

ボリュームのある本を読み切る

　とはいえ、一冊がものすごく分厚いため、全三冊を読み終えるのはかなり大変なことでした。しかし、読み終わった後の充実感や克服感は忘れがたいものとして今でも僕の中に残っています。

　一度ボリュームのある本を読み切ると、それが自分の英語への自信にもつながります。

18 ジェーン・エア

難易度 ★★★

運命に立ち向かう女性を描いた、ゴシックロマンの長編ラブストーリー

> 原題 Jane Eyre
> 著者 Charlotte Brontë
> 発表 1847年
>
> あらすじ：孤児ジェーン・エアは伯母リード夫人の家で虐待されて育つ。十歳のときに送られた学校で恩師のテンプル先生や親友ヘレン・バーンズと出会い、そこで八年間過ごした後、ソーンフィールド邸で家庭教師として雇われる。当主ロチェスター氏と恋に落ちたジェーンは、ためらいながらも求愛を受け入れる。しかし結婚式の当日、衝撃的な事実が判明。ジェーンは運命の渦に巻き込まれていく。

イギリス版「おしん」のようなストーリー

『嵐が丘』（54ページ）の作者エミリー・ブロンテの姉、シャーロット・ブロンテ（Charlotte Brontë）による長編小説です。十九世紀イギリス社会において、不遇な生い立ちの中でたくましく生きる主人公ジェーンは新しい女性像を生み出し、当時大きな反響を呼び起こしました。

幼いときに両親を亡くした孤児の少女ジェーン・エアは、義理の伯母であるリード夫人の家、ゲーツヘッド邸に引き取られます。冷たい伯母やその子供たちに愛されることはなく、つらい境遇の下に暮らしていました。

　ある冷たい雨が降る冬の午後、ジェーンは本棚にあった挿し絵のたくさん入った本を持って秘密の隠れ家である食堂の出窓にこもり、ページをめくっていました。この静かな時間は、しかし、いじわるな従兄妹たちによってあっという間に引き裂かれてしまいます。 **Scene1**

　十四歳にしては大柄でぶくぶく太った従兄のジョン・リードが、本をつかんで四つ年下のジェーンに投げつけたのでした。よけそこねたジェーンは、倒れた拍子にドアに頭を打ちつけて血がしたたり落ちます。躍りかかってきたジョンに髪の毛と肩をつかまれ、ジェーンは必死に抵抗しますが、従姉妹たちの通報で駆けつけた伯母の怒りを買い、二階の薄気味の悪い部屋に閉じ込められてしまいます。 **Scene2**

　冷え切った暗い部屋の中で、ジョン・リードの乱暴な仕打ちや、その妹たちの高慢なよそよそしさ、伯母の自分に対する嫌悪、召し使いたちのえこひいきなどに傷ついたジェーンは、なぜ自分がいつもいじめられていなければならないのだろうと、その不条理

Jane Eyre | 43

と不公平さに苦しみます。

 Scene3 は、大人になったジェーンの視点で、当時の自分の置かれた立場や、子供らしい無邪気さを欠く自らの性質が、ゲーツヘッド邸の人々に相容れなかったことなどを回想する場面です。

学校で得た初めての友人ヘレン

ジェーンを持てあました伯母は、ついに彼女を孤児の養育で知られる学校ローウッドへ預けることにします。つらい日々を送ったリード家から離れることを喜んだジェーンでしたが、ローウッドの学校生活は必要以上に厳しい規律で縛られた過酷なものでした。真冬には室内の水でも凍ってしまうような気温の中、ようやく生き抜けるだけの食事だけを与えられる毎日。

しかし、そのような環境の中でも、彼女は初めての友人ヘレン・バーンズや尊敬するテンプル先生と出会い、しだいに未来に対する希望や、学ぶことの楽しさを感じ始めるようになるのでした。

「汝の敵を愛せよ」というキリストの教えを手本にするようにと言うヘレンに対し、ジェーンは虐げられた少女時代を告白します。そして、リード夫人や従兄のジョンを愛することなど決してできないことを、この聡明な友人に訴えます。 Scene4 では、ジェーンの告白を聞いたヘレン・バーンズの言葉が語られます。ジェー

ンは友人を通じて初めて信仰心というものを知りますが、ヘレンは間もなく病気でこの世を去ってしまいます。

運命を切り開いていく「女性らしさ」

　僕がこの作品を読んで一番に感じたのは、「女性らしさ」に対する西洋と日本の考え方の違いです。この作品が書かれたのは、1847年、日本ではまだ江戸時代です。当時の日本では、まだまだ女性が一人で生きていける道はほとんどありませんでした。そのような時代に、すでにイギリスでは女性が自らの運命を切り開いていくことができていた。そのことに、まず素直に驚きました。

　日本人の考える「女性らしさ」は、もっと弱々しくウェットです。最近になって、ようやく変わってきたのかもしれませんが、従来の日本の「女性らしさ」には、ジェーンのように自ら運命に立ち向かっていくような勇敢さや、独立の気概は求められてきませんでした。

　英語という言語には、そもそもあまり性差がありません。せりふを一行抜き出してみたところで、それが男性のせりふなのか、女性のものなのかはわかりません。そのことを一つ取ってみても、日本における「女性らしさ」「男性らしさ」と西洋のそれが、かなり異なる基盤の上に成り立っていることがわかります。

ある一つの言語を学ぶということは、その世界が持つ「ものの見方」や、言語化することができない社会の「暗黙知(あんもくち)」のようなものまで理解するということではないでしょうか。

愛するロチェスター氏の秘密
　ジェーンは八年間過ごしたローウッドの学校で優秀な成績を収めた後、独立することを決心します。世間から隔絶された規律だらけの狭い世界を飛び出し、新たな自由を求める気持ちに駆られ、ジェーンは新聞広告で家庭教師の口を募って学校を去ることを決意するのです。

　ここまでがジェーンの少女時代で物語の導入部分とも言えます。その後、家庭教師として住み込むことになった家の当主、ロチェスター氏との恋愛がこの物語の主要なテーマになっていきますが、ただそこも甘いだけではなく、奇妙なホラーめいた設定になっています。

　実はこの小説は、ホラーめいたゴシックロマン的要素も含んだ作品です。ロチェスター氏の抱える家庭の秘密、それが次第に明らかになっていくわけですが……。ここではこれ以上は明かさずにおきましょう。

　しかしそういった側面はあるにしても、この作品における女性

の描かれ方はとても現代的であり、十九世紀の段階でこうした女性の生き方の手本となる「ロールモデル」を提示できていたという意味では、非常に感銘を受けた小説と言えます。エンターテインメント小説としても十分楽しめますので、一度チャレンジしてみてはいかがでしょうか。

Jane Eyre

ジェーン・エア

Scene1　CD3 13

"What were you doing behind the curtain?" he asked.

"I was reading."

"Show the book."

I returned to the window and fetched it thence.

"You have no business to take our books; you are a dependent, mama says; you have no money; your father left you none; you ought to beg, and not to live here with gentlemen's children like us, and eat the same meals we do, and wear clothes at our mama's expense. Now, I'll teach you to rummage my bookshelves: for they *are* mine; all the house belongs to me, or will do in a few years. Go and stand by the door, out of the way of the mirror and the windows."

I did so, not at first aware what was his intention;

but when I saw him lift and poise the book and stand in act to hurl it, I instinctively started aside with a cry of alarm: not soon enough, however; the volume was flung, it hit me, and I fell, striking my head against the door and cutting it. The cut bled, the pain was sharp; my terror had passed its climax; other feelings succeeded.

"Wicked and cruel boy!" I said. "You are like a murderer—you are like a slave-driver—you are like the Roman emperors!"

Scene2 CD3 14

"What! what!" he cried. "Did you say that to me? Did you hear her, Eliza and Georgiana? Won't I tell mama? but first"—

He ran headlong at me: I felt him grasp my hair and my shoulder: he had closed with a desperate thing. I really saw in him a tyrant: a murderer. I felt a drop or two of blood from my head trickle down my neck, and was sensible of somewhat pungent sufferings: these sensations for the time predominated over fear, and I received him in frantic sort. I don't very well know what I did with my hands, but he called "Rat! rat!" and bellowed out aloud. Aid was near him: Eliza and Georgiana had run for Mrs. Reed, who was gone upstairs; she now came upon the scene, followed by Bessie and her maid Abbot. We were parted: I heard the words: —

"Dear! dear! What a fury to fly at Master John!"
"Did ever anybody see such a picture of passion!"
Then Mrs. Reed subjoined: —
"Take her away to the red-room, and lock her in there." Four hands were immediately laid upon me, and I was borne upstairs.

Scene 3

I was a discord in Gateshead Hall; I was like nobody there; I had nothing in harmony with Mrs. Reed or her children, or her chosen vassalage. If they did not love me, in fact, as little did I love them. They were not bound to regard with affection a thing that could not sympathise with one amongst them; a heterogeneous thing, opposed to them in temperament, in capacity, in propensities; a useless thing, incapable of serving their interest, or adding to their pleasure; a noxious thing, cherishing the germs of indignation at their treatment, of contempt of their judgment. I know that had I been a sanguine, brilliant, careless, exacting, handsome, romping child—though equally dependent and friendless—Mrs. Reed would have endured my presence more complacently; her children would have entertained for me more of the cordiality of fellow-feeling; the servants would have been less prone to make me the scapegoat of the nursery.

Scene4

"Well," I asked impatiently, "is not Mrs. Reed a hard-hearted, bad woman?"

"She has been unkind to you, no doubt; because, you see, she dislikes your cast of character, as Miss Scatcherd does mine: but how minutely you remember all she has done and said to you! What a singularly deep impression her injustice seems to have made on your heart! No ill-usage so brands its record on my feelings. Would you not be happier if you tried to forget her severity, together with the passionate emotions it excited? Life appears to me too short to be spent in nursing animosity, or registering wrongs.

We are, and must be, one and all, burdened with faults in this world: but the time will soon come when, I trust, we shall put them off in putting off our corruptible bodies; when debasement and sin will fall from us with this cumbrous frame of flesh, and only the spark of the spirit will remain, —the impalpable principle of life and thought, pure as when it left the Creator to inspire the creature: whence it came it will return; perhaps again to be communicated to some being higher than man—perhaps to pass through gradations of glory, from the pale human soul to brighten to the seraph!"

19 嵐が丘

難易度 ★★★

キャサリンとヒースクリフの異常なまでの愛憎を描いた名作

原題	Wuthering Heights
著者	Emily Jane Brontë
発表	1847年

あらすじ：少年ヒースクリフは荒野に立つ屋敷「嵐が丘」の主人に拾われる。彼は屋敷の娘キャサリンと愛し合いながらも、身分の違いから結ばれず、キャサリンはハンサムで金持ちのエドガーと結婚してしまう。ヒースクリフと夫の間で揺れ動くキャサリンは、錯乱の末、娘を出産してこの世を去る。しかし、ヒースクリフの復讐心はとどまることを知らず、子供たちの世代を巻き込んでいく。

"異常"と酷評された名作

小説『嵐が丘』（Wuthering Heights）はとてつもないパワーを秘めた作品です。作者はエミリー・ブロンテ（Emily Brontë）。英文学史上の奇跡と謳われるブロンテ姉妹の一人、『ジェーン・エア』のシャーロット・ブロンテの妹です。イギリスのヨークシャーという当時の文壇からは遠く離れた地で、しかも女性が文学作品

を書くこと自体が珍しかった時代に、ブロンテの三姉妹、シャーロット、エミリー、アンはそれぞれ英文学史に残る傑作を残しました。

エミリーは二十九歳のときにこの作品を出版すると、一年後にはその孤独な生涯を終えます。『嵐が丘』は彼女の生前、"異常な"小説として酷評され、顧みられることはありませんでした。ロマンチックな純愛物語と言うにはあまりにも極端で観念的であり、ヒースクリフが亡霊と対話するシーンなどは狂気めいているため、当時は理解を得られなかったのも不思議はありません。しかし二十世紀に入ると、人間の実存を探求する作品として、シェイクスピアの『リア王』などと並ぶ名作と称されるまでになりました。

ヒースクリフの壮絶な復讐劇

『嵐が丘』は、ヨークシャーの荒野を舞台に主人公のキャサリンとヒースクリフが繰り広げる壮絶な復讐劇です。幼なじみの二人は子供の頃から仲が良く、精神的な結びつきを感じていますが、キャサリンの兄は孤児のヒースクリフを何かにつけ毛嫌いし、父親が病気で亡くなるとヒースクリフを召使いの身分に落としてしまいます。

やがて美しい娘に成長したキャサリンは、ハンサムで金持ちの

エドガー・リントンに結婚を申し込まれます。わがままで気位の高いキャサリンは物語の語り手である家政婦のネリーに、求婚を受け入れたことを伝えます。 Scene1 は、キャサリンが自分の判断が正しかったかどうかをネリーに尋ねた後の場面です。ここでの一人称 "I" は、ネリーを指します。

ネリーはある意味で、この物語の中で一番「常識的な感覚を持った」人物です。キャサリンの浅はかさを非難しつつ「今だけが問題なのなら、エドガーさまと結婚なさい」と答えます。しかしキャサリンは「言われなくてもそうするわ」と言いながらも、自分が間違っていることはわかっていると言い放つのです。 Scene2

キャサリンがエドガーと結婚することを知ったヒースクリフは館を飛び出し、行方をくらまします。そして月日が流れ、三年が過ぎたある日のこと、見違えるように立派な紳士になったヒースクリフが、今は幸せな結婚生活を築いているキャサリンの元を訪ねてきます。

穏やかな性質の夫エドガーの前で、キャサリンはヒースクリフの帰郷を手放しで喜びますが、紳士を装ったヒースクリフの長い復讐劇が、ここから始まるのでした。 Scene3

キャサリンの死後、明かされる謎

　この物語では、とても長い年月が描かれています。主人公の一人であるキャサリンが死に、その娘キャシーとヒースクリフの息子の代まで、「ヒースクリフとキャサリンの物語」はずっと続いていきます。読み進めるにつれ、ヒースクリフがキャサリンの忘れ形見キャシーのことを愛してしまったのではないかと思わせる場面もありますが、最後に大どんでん返しが待っています。そこでヒースクリフの残虐な行為の謎が、ようやく明らかになるのです。

　非常にスピリチュアルな面がある作品でもあり、ヒースクリフがキャサリンの亡霊と会話をしているところなどは圧巻で、思わず背筋が寒くなります。

　こういう一風変わった作品は、改めて英語というものの奥行きの深さを感じさせます。僕たちはどうしても、英語というと学校で習うような、あるいはビジネスシーンで使うような「実践的な」アメリカ英語をイメージしがちですが、英語の本当の味わい深さはこのような文学作品にあるのではないでしょうか。

Wuthering Heights

嵐が丘

Scene 1

"There are many things to be considered, before that question can be answered properly," I said sententiously. "First and foremost, do you love Mr. Edgar?"

"Who can help it? Of course I do," she answered. Then I put her through the following catechism—for a girl of twenty-two it was not injudicious.

"Why do you love him, Miss Cathy?"

"Nonsense, I do—that's sufficient."

"By no means; you must say why?"

"Well, because he is handsome, and pleasant to be with."

"Bad," was my commentary.

"And because he is young and cheerful."

"Bad, still."

"And, because he loves me."

"Indifferent, coming there."

"And he will be rich, and I shall like to be the greatest woman of the neighbourhood, and I shall be proud of having such a husband."

"Worst of all! And, now, say how you love him?"

"As everybody loves—You're silly, Nelly."

"Not at all—Answer."

"I love the ground under his feet, and the air over his head, and everything he touches, and every word he says—I love all his looks, and all his actions, and him entirely, and altogether. There now!"

"And why?"

"Nay—you are making a jest of it; it is exceedingly ill-natured! It's no jest to me!" said the young lady, scowling and turning her face to the fire.

"I'm very far from jesting, Miss Catherine," I replied, "you love Mr. Edgar, because he is handsome, and young, and cheerful, and rich, and loves you. The last, however, goes for nothing—You would love him without that, probably, and with it, you wouldn't, unless he possessed the four former attractions."

"No, to be sure not—I should only pity him—hate him, perhaps, if he were ugly, and a clown."

"But, there are several other handsome, rich young men in the world; handsomer, possibly, and richer than he is—What should hinder you from loving them?"

"If there be any, they are out of my way—I've seen none like Edgar."

"You may see some; and he won't always be handsome, and young, and may not always be rich."

"He is now; and I have only to do with the present

—I wish you would speak rationally."

"Well, that settles it—if you have only to do with the present, marry Mr. Linton."

Scene2

"If I were in heaven, Nelly, I should be extremely miserable."

"Because you are not fit to go there," I answered. "All sinners would be miserable in heaven."

"But it is not for that. I dreamt, once, that I was there."

"I tell you I won't hearken to your dreams, Miss Catherine! I'll go to bed," I interrupted again.

She laughed, and held me down, for I made a motion to leave my chair.

"This is nothing," cried she; "I was only going to say that heaven did not seem to be my home; and I broke my heart with weeping to come back to earth; and the angels were so angry that they flung me out, into the middle of the heath on the top of Wuthering Heights; where I woke sobbing for joy. That will do to explain my secret, as well as the other. I've no more business to marry Edgar Linton than I have to be in heaven; and if the wicked man in there had not brought Heathcliff so low, I shouldn't have thought of it. It would degrade me to marry Heathcliff, now; so he shall never know how I love him; and that, not because he's handsome, Nelly, but because he's more myself than I am. Whatever our souls are made of, his and mine are the same, and Linton's is as different as a moonbeam from lightning, or frost from fire."

Ere this speech ended I became sensible of Heathcliff's presence. Having noticed a slight movement, I turned my head, and saw him rise from the bench, and steal out, noiselessly. He had listened till he heard Catherine say it would degrade her to marry him, and then he staid to hear no farther.

Scene 3

"Sit down, sir," he said, at length. "Mrs. Linton, recalling old times, would have me give you a cordial reception, and, of course, I am gratified when anything occurs to please her."

"And I also," answered Heathcliff, "especially if it be anything in which I have a part. I shall stay an hour or two willingly."

He took a seat opposite Catherine, who kept her gaze fixed on him as if she feared he would vanish were she to remove it. He did not raise his to her, often; a quick glance now and then sufficed; but it flashed back, each time more confidently, the undisguised delight he drank from hers.

They were too much absorbed in their mutual joy to suffer embarrassment; not so Mr. Edgar: he grew pale with pure annoyance, a feeling that reached its climax when his lady rose—and stepping across the rug, seized Heathcliff's hands again, and laughed like one beside herself.

"I shall think it a dream to-morrow!" she cried. "I shall not be able to believe that I have seen, and touched, and spoken to you once more—and yet, cruel Heathcliff! you don't deserve this welcome. To be absent and silent for three years, and never to think of me!"

"A little more than you have thought of me!" he murmured. "I heard of your marriage, Cathy, not long since; and, while waiting in the yard below, I meditated this plan—just to have one glimpse of your face—a stare of surprise, perhaps, and pretended pleasure; afterwards settle my score with Hindley; and then prevent the law by doing execution on myself. Your welcome has put these ideas out of my mind; but beware of meeting me with another aspect next time! Nay, you'll not drive me off again—you were really sorry for me, were you? Well, there was cause. I've fought through a bitter life since I last heard your voice, and you must forgive me, for I struggled only for you!"

20 高慢と偏見

難易度 ★★☆

十九世紀イギリスの恋愛と結婚を、鋭い心理描写でテンポよく描く

原題 Pride and Prejudice
著者 Jane Austen
発表 1813年

あらすじ：イギリスの田舎町ロンボーンに独身の資産家ビングリーが引っ越してくる。五人の娘を抱えるベネット家の母親は、娘たちに条件のよい結婚をさせようと躍起になる。母親がもっとも期待をかける長女ジェインはビングリーといい雰囲気になるものの、別れてしまう。一方、次女エリザベスとビングリーの友人ダーシーは、誤解と偏見によって対立しながらも次第に惹かれあっていく。

田舎町にやってきた、騒動の種

『高慢と偏見』(Pride and Prejudice) はイギリスの女性作家、ジェイン・オースティン (Jane Austen) の長編恋愛小説です。物語の舞台はイギリスのとある田舎町。ロンドンのような都会とは違い、毎日がのんびりと過ぎていくこの平和な町では、人々の関心事はもっぱら他人の恋愛や結婚の話です。

当時、女性が仕事を持って自立することは、ほとんどありませんでした。ですから、女性が生活レベルを維持しながら生きていくためには、自分より少しでも上の階級の男に嫁ぐことが唯一の道とされていた時代だったのです。

　主人公のエリザベス・ベネットは五人姉妹の次女。聡明でユーモア溢れるしっかり者です。姉妹の母親は、ベネット家の近くに引っ越してきたハンサムでお金持ちのビングリー氏を、長女ジェインの結婚相手にと目をつけます。

　娘たちを上流階級の家に嫁がせたい母親は、ビングリー氏とお近づきになるために必死になります。 Scene1 は、ベネット家の人々が舞踏会でビングリー氏に初めて会う場面です。ビングリーは明るく気さくな青年で、たちまち周囲の人と打ち解けます。しかし、彼の友人のダーシー氏はビングリーを上回る美男子で大富豪なのですが、お高くとまった鼻持ちならない高慢な人物として、周囲の反感を買います。

エリザベスの憎しみと恋心

　エリザベスもまた、ダーシーのことをイヤな奴と思い、嫌うようになります。 Scene2 は後日、エリザベスとダーシーの間で交わされる、なかなかスリリングな会話です。エリザベスは「ダー

シーさんには欠点がない」と皮肉たっぷりに言いますが、意外にもダーシーは「僕はたくさん欠点を持っています」と、自らの性格について冷静に語るのでした。

　エリザベスとダーシーの関係とは反対に、ビングリーと長女ジェインは互いに好意を持ち、周囲は二人が結婚するものと思っていましたが、ダーシーのせいで二人は別れてしまいます。ダーシーにとっては当時の身分制度と慣習に則った考えから、彼なりに親友を思っての行動でしたが、姉思いのエリザベスはこのことを知って激怒します。

　ところが、そのダーシーは少しずつエリザベスに惹かれていくのでした。 Scene3 は、ダーシーが彼女に愛を告白する場面です。「身分違いの恋ゆえ、なかなかプロポーズに踏み切れなかった」と言うダーシーに対して、エリザベスは怒りで顔を真っ赤にしながら、その申し出をぴしゃりと断ります。ダーシーは必死に冷静さを装いながら、自分はうそが嫌いで「身分違いの恋に悩んだことはまったく恥じていない」と告げます。エリザベスはさらに厳しい言葉で彼を拒絶したため、ダーシーは「わかりました。もう十分です」と言い、部屋を出ていきます。こうして二人は決裂してしまいます。 Scene4

　物語の後半、二人は思いがけない場所で再会し、さらにエリザ

ベスの妹リディアが男と駆け落ちするという事件が起きたため、ストーリーは思わぬ展開を遂げます。

ぐいぐいと引き込む心理描写

この作品は主人公エリザベスの視点で、それぞれの登場人物たちの内面が、その愛すべき点も卑小(わいしょう)さもひっくるめて、細やかに描かれています。人間の意地の悪さ、凡庸さ、醜さを顕微鏡で内面を覗いているようにリアルに描き、読者をぐいぐいと物語に引き込んでいきます。そして、誰の心にもある「高慢と偏見」を決して美化することなく、愛で包み込む。それこそが、オースティン作品の最大の魅力だと思います。

Pride and Prejudice

Scene1

Mr. Bingley was good looking and gentlemanlike; he had a pleasant countenance, and easy, unaffected manners. His sisters were fine women, with an air of decided fashion. His brother-in-law, Mr. Hurst, merely looked the gentleman; but his friend Mr. Darcy soon drew the attention of the room by his fine, tall person, handsome features, noble mien; and the report which was in general circulation within five minutes after his entrance, of his having ten thousand a year. The gentlemen pronounced him to be a fine figure of a man, the ladies declared he was much handsomer than Mr. Bingley, and he was looked at with great admiration for about half the evening, till his manners gave a disgust which turned the tide of his popularity; for he was discovered to be proud, to be above his company, and above being pleased; and not all his large estate in Derbyshire could then save him from having a most forbidding, disagreeable countenance, and being unworthy to be compared with his friend.

Scene2

"I am perfectly convinced by it that Mr. Darcy has no defect. He owns it himself without disguise."

"No"—said Darcy, "I have made no such pretension. I have faults enough, but they are not, I hope, of understanding. My temper I dare not vouch for.—It is I believe too little yielding—certainly too little for the convenience of the world. I cannot forget the follies and vices of others so soon as I ought, nor their offences against myself. My feelings are not

Pride and Prejudice | 71

puffed about with every attempt to move them. My temper would perhaps be called resentful.—My good opinion once lost is lost forever."

"*That* is a failing indeed!"—cried Elizabeth. "Implacable resentment *is* a shade in a character. But you have chosen your fault well.—I really cannot *laugh* at it. You are safe from me."

"There is, I believe, in every disposition a tendency to some particular evil, a natural defect, which not even the best education can overcome."

"And *your* defect is a propensity to hate everybody."

"And yours," he replied with a smile, "is willfully to misunderstand them."

Scene3

He sat down for a few moments, and then getting up

walked about the room. Elizabeth was surprised, but said not a word. After a silence of several minutes he came towards her in an agitated manner, and thus began,

"In vain have I struggled. It will not do. My feelings will not be repressed. You must allow me to tell you how ardently I admire and love you."

Elizabeth's astonishment was beyond expression. She stared, coloured, doubted, and was silent. This he considered sufficient encouragement, and the avowal of all that he felt and had long felt for her, immediately followed. He spoke well, but there were feelings besides those of the heart to be detailed, and he was not more eloquent on the subject of tenderness than of pride. His sense of her inferiority—of its being a degradation—of the family obstacles which judgment had always opposed to inclination, were

Pride and Prejudice

dwelt on with a warmth which seemed due to the consequence he was wounding, but was very unlikely to recommend his suit.

Scene4

Elizabeth felt herself growing more angry every moment; yet she tried to the utmost to speak with composure when she said,

"You are mistaken, Mr. Darcy, if you suppose that the mode of your declaration affected me in any other way, than as it spared me the concern which I might have felt in refusing you, had you behaved in a more gentleman-like manner."

She saw him start at this, but he said nothing, and she continued,

"You could not have made me the offer of your hand in any possible way that would have tempted me to accept it."

Again his astonishment was obvious; and he looked at her with an expression of mingled incredulity and mortification. She went on.

"From the very beginning, from the first moment I may almost say, of my acquaintance with you, your manners impressing me with the fullest belief of your arrogance, your conceit, and your selfish disdain of the feelings of others, were such as to form that ground-work of disapprobation, on which succeeding events have built so immovable a dislike; and I had not known you a month before I felt that you were the last man in the world whom I could ever be prevailed on to marry."

"You have said quite enough, madam. I perfectly comprehend your feelings, and have now only to be ashamed of what my own have been. Forgive me for having taken up so much of your time, and accept my best wishes for your health and happiness."

And with these words he hastily left the room, and Elizabeth heard him the next moment open the front door and quit the house.

The tumult of her mind was now painfully great. She knew not how to support herself, and from actual weakness sat down and cried for half an hour. Her astonishment, as she reflected on what had passed, was increased by every review of it. That she should receive an offer of marriage from Mr. Darcy! that he should have been in love with her for so many months! so much in love as to wish to marry her in spite of all the objections which had made him prevent his friend's marrying her sister, and which must appear at least with equal force in his own case, was almost incredible! it was gratifying to have inspired unconsciously so strong an affection.

Column
古典文学の天才、シェイクスピアの戯曲に挑戦

"辞書"として使える、膨大な語彙

　イギリスの戯曲家シェイクスピアは、音楽界におけるモーツァルトと同様、間違いなく「天才」と呼べる人物です。

　今でこそ、文学界の巨匠としてその名を世界にとどろかせていますが、当時の彼はロンドンっ子の求めるまま、グローブ座で上演する作品を次々に生み出していかなければならない一劇作家でした。いつまでも同じ作品を上演していたのでは大衆の関心は離れていきます。一作ごとにじっくりと構成を練るような時間はなく、いわば"自転車操業的"に新作を作り続けていたはずです。

　にもかかわらず、彼の作品群の完成度、深い人間観察、韻文の美しさは比類なく、その世界の深さや広がりは驚くべきものがあります。英語表現一つとっても、彼の作品の中で使われている語彙は膨大なものです。その国の言語を多彩に織り込ませて"辞書"としても扱える作品こそが、国民文学と呼べるのですが、その意味におい

てシェイクスピアの作品はまさにイングランドの国民文学と呼ぶにふさわしいものです。

翻訳では味わえない、シェイクスピアの魅力

そんなシェイクスピアの作品の中で、どれが最も優れているか、あるいはどの作品を個人的に一番好きか、一つの作品を挙げるのは極めて難しいものです。

『ハムレット』を読めば、やはり主人公のハムレットが口にする有名な台詞 "To be, or not to be: that is the question." や、彼がオフィーリアに向かって放つ「尼寺へ行け！」が思い浮かびます。あるいは『マクベス』で魔女が謎解きのように言う、"Fair is foul, and foul is fair." も印象的です。

僕がシェイクスピアを読み進めていったのは、高校生の頃でした。彼の英語は古い時代の作品であることも含めて、決して平易なものではありません。そもそも韻を踏んだ戯曲は、その国の言葉を学ぶ外国人が完全に理解しようとするのは難しいのです。

しかし、それくらい奥深いものだからこそ、原文を読むことで創意工夫を凝らした英語表現の素晴らしさ、面白さが伝わってくるのです。あらすじを知っている作品も多いでしょう。一字一句の理解は少なくても、ぜひ一度、原文でチャレンジしてみてください。

21 ガーデン・パーティー

難易度 ★★★

一枚の絵のように美しい、
少女の感受性のゆらめきを描いた作品

> **原題** The Garden Party
> **著者** Katherine Mansfield
> **発表** 1922年
>
> あらすじ：裕福なローラの家では、その日行われるガーデン・パーティーの準備が慌ただしく進められている。そんなとき、近所に住む貧しい男の事故死が伝えられる。ローラは亡くなった男の家のすぐ近くで華やかなパーティーをすることをためらい、中止しようと提案するが、周囲は耳を傾けてくれない。パーティーは盛況に終わり、ローラの母親は残ったごちそうを遺族に届けてやりなさいと言う。ローラは違和感を抱きながら、亡くなった男の家を訪問する。

僕にとっての"完璧な小説"

『ガーデン・パーティー』(The Garden Party)は、短いながらも、非常に優れた短編小説です。三十四歳の若さでこの世を去ったニュージーランド生まれの女性作家、キャサリン・マンスフィールドの代表作です。

僕は最初に読んだときも衝撃を受けましたが、今回改めて読み

直してみても、やはり"完璧な小説"だと感じます。おそらく現代においてこういう作品を書くことができたら、即座に芥川賞を取れるのではないでしょうか。

パーティーを準備する高揚感

　主人公は裕福な家庭のお嬢さんローラ。彼女の家では今日、ガーデン・パーティーが開かれようとしています。あつらえたような雲一つない晴天。朝から台所では料理が準備され、注文した花やお菓子が次々と運び込まれてきます。庭には楽団が来て演奏することになっています。

　今年は子どもたちに段取りをまかせようと決めている母親は、ローラに天幕を張る場所を指揮するように言います。 Scene1
ローラはバターを塗ったパンを持ったまま、浮き立った気分で庭に出ていき、そこで天幕を運び込んできた職人たちと言葉を交わします。彼女は、自分の階級より下の人間と言葉を交わすことにまだ慣れていません。母親のように鷹揚に「おはよう」と言ってみたものの、恥ずかしくなりどもってしまいます。

　そんな彼女に若い職人たちは感じよく笑いかけ、優しく接してくれます。自分としては「馬鹿げた階級差別」意識など、少しも感じない。そう心の中でつぶやき、ローラは一番背の高い男がラ

ベンダーの匂いをかぐのを見て、心をときめかせます。 `Scene2`

　これからパーティーが始まろうとしている心躍るような情景描写と、ローラの豊かな観察眼、感受性のゆらめきが手に取るようにわかる場面です。

少女の心を揺るがす「事件」

　着々とパーティーの準備が進む中、ある事件のニュースがこの家にもたらされます。家のすぐ近くの、貧しい階級の人々が暮らす地域で、若い男が事故で亡くなったというのです。あとには妻と幼い五人の子供が残されたといいます。ローラは即座にパーティーの中止を訴えますが、姉のジョーズはパーティーを彼らのために止めるなどとんでもないことだと反対します。 `Scene3`

　家のすぐ近くに亡くなった人がいるというのに、ガーデン・パーティーをするなんて……。ローラは興奮して母親の部屋に駆け込みますが、真剣にとりあってもらえません。 `Scene4`

「あんたが今やろうとしているように、皆にとって楽しいことを台なしにしてしまうのは、それこそ、思いやりのあることじゃないわね」

　母親にこう言われ、ローラは戸惑いながらも従います。パーティーがすっかりすんだら、もう一度考え直してみよう……。しか

しパーティーが始まればその楽しそうな雰囲気に惹かれ、ローラはおいしい料理や美しい衣装、華やかな会話のひとときを楽しみます。

　無事パーティーが終わり一息ついたところで、残った料理を見た母親は、ローラに向かって、この残ったごちそうを遺族に届けてやりなさいと提案します。彼女は違和感を抱きながらも、パーティーのドレスを着たままバスケットにごちそうを詰めて、事故で亡くなった人の家を訪れます。

　クライマックスのシーンは、とても繊細なニュアンスで静かに描かれており、読む人々の胸に響きます。会話も多く読みやすく、それでいて美しいこの作品は、英語で読んでこそ、その良さを味わうことができるのではないかと思います。

The Garden Party

ガーデン・パーティー

Scene1

And after all the weather was ideal. They could not have had a more perfect day for a garden party if they had ordered it. Windless, warm, the sky without a cloud. Only the blue was veiled with a haze of light gold, as it is sometimes in early summer. The gardener had been up since dawn, mowing the lawns and sweeping them, until the grass and the dark flat rosettes where the daisy plants had been seemed to shine. As for the roses, you could not help feeling they understood that roses are the only flowers that impress people at garden parties; the only flowers that everybody is certain of knowing. Hundreds, yes, literally hundreds, had come out in a single night; the green bushes bowed down as though they had been visited by archangels.

Breakfast was not yet over before the men came to put up the marquee.

"Where do you want the marquee put, mother?"

"My dear child, it's no use asking me. I'm determined to leave everything to you children this year. Forget I am your mother. Treat me as an honoured guest."

But Meg could not possibly go and supervise the men. She had washed her hair before breakfast, and she sat drinking her coffee in a green turban, with a dark wet curl stamped on each cheek. Jose, the butterfly, always came down in a silk petticoat and a kimono jacket.

"You'll have to go, Laura; you're the artistic one."

Away Laura flew, still holding her piece of bread-and-butter. It's so delicious to have an excuse for eating out of doors, and besides, she loved having to arrange things; she always felt she could do it so much better than anybody else.

Scene2

"Look here, miss, that's the place. Against those trees. Over there. That'll do fine."

Against the karakas. Then the karaka-trees would be hidden. And they were so lovely, with their broad, gleaming leaves, and their clusters of yellow fruit. They were like trees you imagined growing on a desert island, proud, solitary, lifting their leaves and fruits to the sun in a kind of silent splendour. Must they be hidden by a marquee?

They must. Already the men had shouldered their staves and were making for the place. Only the tall fellow was left. He bent down, pinched a sprig of lavender, put his thumb and forefinger to his nose and snuffed up the smell. When Laura saw that gesture she forgot all about the karakas in her wonder at him caring for things like that—caring for the smell of lavender. How many men that she knew would have done such a thing. Oh, how extraordinarily nice workmen were, she thought. Why couldn't she have workmen for friends rather than the silly boys she danced with and who came to Sunday night supper? She would get on much better with men like these.

It's all the fault, she decided, as the tall fellow drew something on the back of an envelope, something that was to be looped up or left to hang, of these absurd class distinctions. Well, for her part, she didn't feel them. Not a bit, not an atom… And now there came the chock-chock of wooden hammers. Some one whistled, some one sang out, "Are you right there, matey?" "Matey!" The friendliness of it, the—the—Just to prove how happy she was, just to show the tall fellow how at home she felt, and how she despised stupid conventions, Laura took a big bite of her bread-and-butter as she stared at the little drawing. She felt just like a work-girl.

Scene3 CD3 26

"What's the matter? What's happened?"

"There's been a horrible accident," said cook. "A man killed."

"A man killed! Where? How? When?"

But Godber's man wasn't going to have his story snatched from under his very nose.

"Know those little cottages just below here, miss?" Know them? Of course, she knew them. "Well, there's a young chap living there, name of Scott, a carter. His horse shied at a traction-engine, corner of Hawke

Street this morning, and he was thrown out on the back of his head. Killed."

"Dead!" Laura stared at Godber's man.

"Dead when they picked him up," said Godber's man with relish. "They were taking the body home as I come up here." And he said to the cook, "He's left a wife and five little ones."

"Jose, come here." Laura caught hold of her sister's sleeve and dragged her through the kitchen to the other side of the green baize door. There she paused and leaned against it. "Jose!" she said, horrified, "however are we going to stop everything?"

"Stop everything, Laura!" cried Jose in astonishment. "What do you mean?"

"Stop the garden party, of course." Why did Jose pretend?

But Jose was still more amazed. "Stop the garden

The Garden Party | 89

party? My dear Laura, don't be so absurd. Of course we can't do anything of the kind. Nobody expects us to. Don't be so extravagant."

"But we can't possibly have a garden party with a man dead just outside the front gate."

Scene4

"Mother, can I come into your room?" Laura turned the big glass doorknob.

"Of course, child. Why, what's the matter? What's given you such a colour?" And Mrs. Sheridan turned round from her dressing-table. She was trying on a new hat.

"Mother, a man's been killed," began Laura.

"*Not* in the garden?" interrupted her mother.

"No, no!"

"Oh, what a fright you gave me!" Mrs. Sheridan

sighed with relief, and took off the big hat and held it on her knees.

"But listen, mother," said Laura. Breathless, half-choking, she told the dreadful story. "Of course, we can't have our party, can we?" she pleaded. "The band and everybody arriving. They'd hear us, mother; they're nearly neighbours!"

To Laura's astonishment her mother behaved just like Jose; it was harder to bear because she seemed amused. She refused to take Laura seriously.

22 ボーディング・ハウス

難易度 ★★★

『ダブリン市民』の短編で、ジョイスの詩的文学に触れる

> 原題 The Boarding House
> 著者 James Augustine Aloysius Joyce
> 発表 1914年
>
> あらすじ：下宿屋の娘ポリーは、下宿人の男性と恋仲になってしまう。女主人は娘から話を聞き出し、母親として男性に直談判をすることを決意する。母親に二人のことを知られてしまったことを娘に告げられると、男性はまだ独身の自由に未練を持ちながらも、半ば観念してその時を待つ。

ジョイスは文壇のピカソ？

アイルランドが誇る作家、ジェイムズ・ジョイス（James Joyce）の『ダブリン市民』は、僕のお気に入りの一冊です。この短編集にはアイルランドの主都、ダブリンに住む市井の人々の生活模様を、短いスナップショットで切り取った十五編の作品が収録されています。

アイルランドにはもともと、サミュエル・ベケットやオスカー・

ワイルドなど、詩的な作品を書く作家が多いのですが、ジョイスもそのうちの一人で、彼ほど芸術としての英語表現を極めた人物はいないのではないかと思っています。

ジョイスには、有名な『ユリシーズ』や『フィネガンズ・ウェイク』などの長編小説もありますが、後期に書かれたこれらの作品は、あまりに実験小説の色合いが濃すぎて、何が書いてあるのかわからない危険性があります。しかし、初期の作品であるこの『ダブリン市民』はとてもわかりやすい。

そういう意味で、ジョイスは画家のピカソに似ているのかもしれません。ピカソも、後半のキュビズムのような実験的かつ革新的な表現方法で描いた絵が有名ですが、若い頃の習作などはきわめて正当な手法で描かれており、素人が見てもわかりやすいものです。ピカソの父親も画家でしたが、若い息子の描く絵を見て、自らは絵筆を置いたとも言われているくらいです。

授業で読んだ「ボーディング・ハウス」

さて、僕は大学一年生のとき、授業でこの『ダブリン市民』の中の短編「ボーディング・ハウス」を読みました。ボーディング・ハウスとは、下宿屋という意味です。

その下宿屋を切り盛りしている女主人のミセス・ムーニーは、下

宿している若い男たちから The Madam（やり手女将）と呼ばれています。女主人にはポリーという十九歳の娘がいますが、その娘と下宿している男性が恋仲になってしまいます。 Scene1

　女主人は最初それに目をつむっていますが、時期を見計らって娘から話を聞き出します。母親として娘をしかるべき相手に嫁がせる義務感を持っている彼女は、ついに男性に直談判をすることを決意します。相手の男性、ドーラン氏は三十四、五歳。若気の至りなどという言い訳が通る年齢ではありません。

　 Scene2 は、初夏の晴れた日曜日の朝、女主人が物思いにふける場面です。こういう場合、自分と娘の失った名誉を回復するには、償いはたった一つ——つまり、結婚しかない。女主人は自分の持ち札を確認してから、女中のメアリーをドーラン氏の部屋へやり、話がしたいと伝えます。

　一方、真面目なドーラン氏は娘と関係を持ったことを周囲に知られてしまった以上、今となっては結婚するか逃げるしかないと不安でたまりません。 Scene3

　ポリーは彼に、母親が二人のことを知ってしまったことを告げに来ます。まだ独身ならではの自由な生活に未練のあるドーラン氏は、娘を愛しているかどうか決心がつかないまま、半ば義務感から観念してその時を待ちます。

独特の余韻があるラストシーン

　ラストシーンは独特の余韻を残して終わります。やはり、ジョイスの文章は英語における散文表現の最高峰の一つと言えるでしょう。この「ボーディング・ハウス」以外にも『ダブリンの市民』の作品はどれもが短くて読みやすいので、ぜひ読んでみてはいかがでしょうか。

The Boarding House

ボーディング・ハウス

Scene1

Polly was a slim girl of nineteen; she had light soft hair and a small full mouth. Her eyes, which were grey with a shade of green through them, had a habit of glancing upwards when she spoke with anyone, which made her look like a little perverse madonna. Mrs. Mooney had first sent her daughter to be a typist in a corn-factor's office but, as a disreputable sheriff's man used to come every other day to the office, asking to be allowed to say a word to his daughter, she had taken her daughter home again and set her to do housework. As Polly was very lively the intention was to give her the run of the young men. Besides, young men like to feel that there is a young woman not very far away. Polly, of course, flirted with the young men but Mrs. Mooney, who was a shrewd judge, knew that the young men were only passing the time away: none of them meant business. Things went on so for a long time and Mrs. Mooney began to think of sending Polly back to typewriting when she noticed that something was going on between Polly and one of the young men. She watched the pair and kept her own counsel.

Scene2

Mrs. Mooney glanced instinctively at the little gilt clock on the mantelpiece as soon as she had become aware through her revery that the bells of George's Church had stopped ringing. It was seventeen minutes past eleven: she would have lots of time to have the matter out with Mr. Doran and then catch short twelve at Marlborough Street. She was sure she would win. To begin with she had all the weight of social opinion on her side: she was an outraged mother. She had allowed him to live beneath her roof, assuming that he was a man of honour, and he had simply abused her hospitality. He was thirty-four or thirty-five years of age, so that youth could not be pleaded as his excuse; nor could ignorance be his excuse since he was a man who had seen something of the world. He had simply taken advantage of Polly's youth and inexperience: that was evident. The question was: What reparation would he make?

Scene3

Mr. Doran was very anxious indeed this Sunday morning. He had made two attempts to shave but his hand had been so unsteady that he had been obliged to desist. Three days' reddish beard fringed his jaws and every two or three minutes a mist gathered on his glasses so that he had to take them off and polish them with his pocket-handkerchief. The recollection of his confession of the night before was a cause of acute pain to him; the priest had drawn out every ridiculous detail of the affair and in the end had so magnified his sin that he was almost thankful at being afforded a loophole of reparation. The harm was done. What could he do now but marry her or run away? He could not brazen it out. The affair would be sure to be talked of and his employer would be certain to hear of it. Dublin is such a small city: everyone knows everyone else's business. He felt his heart leap warmly in his throat as he heard in his excited imagination old Mr. Leonard calling out in his rasping voice: *Send Mr. Doran here, please.*

23 アッシャー家の崩壊

難易度 ★★★

**身の毛もよだつほど怖いながらも、美しい。
ポーの芸術的な短編**

> 原題 The Fall of the House of Usher
> 著者 Edgar Allan Poe
> 発表 1839年
>
> あらすじ：主人公の「私」は、少年時代の友人アッシャーから、体と心の病を軽くするために会いたいと頼まれ、陰鬱で古い屋敷を訪れる。屋敷には重い病を患ったアッシャーの妹、マデリンがいっしょに暮らしていた。ある晩、アッシャーは突然マデリンの死を告げ、アッシャーと私はその亡骸を安置室に納める。数日後の嵐の夜、二人で古い書物を読んでいると、アッシャーは驚くべき言葉を口にする。

アッシャー邸への招待

アメリカの小説家、エドガー・アラン・ポー（Edgar Allan Poe）の「アッシャー家の崩壊」（The Fall of the House of Usher）を、初めて読んだときの戦慄は忘れられません。

世の中には醜いホラーと、美しいホラーが存在すると思うのですが、これは完全に後者のホラーです。この作品は身の毛もよだ

つほど怖いながらも、詩的な美しさがあります。ここまで芸術的に《美》と《恐怖》を同時に描ける作家は、ポーをおいてはいないでしょう。

　物語は、語り手の「私」が少年時代の友人アッシャーから一通の手紙を受け取り、彼の求めるままアッシャー邸を訪ねていく場面から始まります。アッシャーは昔から内気で感受性の鋭い少年でしたが、久々に見る彼は異様な形相でやせ細り、病の床につき精神的にも錯乱ぎみの状態でした。

　アッシャーは自らの病気について、「感覚の病的な過敏性」に悩まされていることを「私」に語ります。ごく淡泊な食べ物しかのどを通らず、特定の生地の衣類しか着られず、花の匂いは耐えがたく、わずかな光に目が痛み、管楽器以外の音には恐怖心を感じると言うのです。 **Scene1**

マデリンの死と、驚くべき結末

　さらにアッシャーは唯一の身内である妹のマデリンが、長い間重い病気を患っており、そのことが自らの病の原因であることを認めます。そのとき「私」は、部屋の奥をよぎるマデリンの姿を目にしますが、恐怖の入り混じった驚きを感じるとともに、それが彼女を見る最後になるだろうと予感します。

The Fall of the House of Usher | 101

「私」は次第に、陰鬱なアッシャー邸に奇妙で狂気めいたものを感じていくのでした。この作品は、屋敷を取り巻く自然や建物などの情景描写にも優れています。短編小説の舞台づくりとして、これほどまで完璧な描写はないのではないかと思います。

　ある晩、アッシャーは突然、マデリンが亡くなったことを伝え、その亡骸を「正式に埋葬する」までの二週間、屋敷の地下室の一つに安置するつもりであると言います。「私」はアッシャーの求めに応じ、彼とともに遺体を棺に納め、地下室の安置所に運びます。

Scene2

　数日が過ぎた頃、アッシャーの精神状態は悪化の様相を呈します。日々の仕事は手につかず、青白い顔がいっそう不気味な色合いを帯び、何時間も虚空を凝視している姿に「私」は不安になります。

Scene3

　そんなある夜のこと、すでに床についていた「私」は本能的な恐怖に促されて飛び起きます。嵐の合間を縫って切れ切れに聞こえてくる、何かの物音。と、そこに蒼白な顔のアッシャーが部屋に入ってきたのです……。

　短い作品ですが、ポーの名作中の名作です。文章は決してやさしくはありませんが、この怖ろしいながらも美しい世界に一度チャレンジしてみてください。

The Fall of the House of Usher

アッシャー家の崩壊

Scene1

To an anomalous species of terror I found him a bounden slave. "I shall perish," said he, "I *must* perish in this deplorable folly. Thus, thus, and not otherwise, shall I be lost. I dread the events of the future, not in themselves, but in their results. I shudder at the thought of any, even the most trivial, incident, which may operate upon this intolerable agitation of soul. I have, indeed, no abhorrence of danger, except in its absolute effect—in terror. In this unnerved—in this pitiable condition—I feel that the period will sooner or later arrive when I must abandon life and reason together, in some struggle with the grim phantasm, FEAR."

I learned, moreover, at intervals, and through

broken and equivocal hints, another singular feature of his mental condition. He was enchained by certain superstitious impressions in regard to the dwelling which he tenanted, and whence, for many years, he had never ventured forth—in regard to an influence whose supposititious force was conveyed in terms too shadowy here to be re-stated—an influence which some peculiarities in the mere form and substance of his family mansion, had, by dint of long sufferance, he said, obtained over his spirit—an effect which the *physique* of the gray walls and turrets, and of the dim tarn into which they all looked down, had, at length, brought about upon the *morale* of his existence.

Scene2 CD3 32

At the request of Usher, I personally aided him in the arrangements for the temporary entombment. The body having been encoffined, we two alone bore it to its rest. The vault in which we placed it (and which had been so long unopened that our torches, half smothered in its oppressive atmosphere, gave us little opportunity for investigation) was small, damp, and entirely without means of admission for light; lying, at great depth, immediately beneath that portion of the building in which was my own sleeping apartment. It had been used, apparently, in remote feudal times, for the worst purposes of a donjon-keep, and, in later days, as a place of deposit for powder, or some other highly combustible substance, as a portion of its floor, and the whole interior of a long archway through which we reached it, were carefully sheathed with copper. The door, of massive iron, had been, also, similarly protected. Its immense weight caused an unusually sharp grating sound, as it moved upon its hinges.

Scene 3

And now, some days of bitter grief having elapsed, an observable change came over the features of the mental disorder of my friend. His ordinary manner had vanished. His ordinary occupations were neglected or forgotten. He roamed from chamber to chamber with hurried, unequal, and objectless step. The pallor of his countenance had assumed, if possible, a more ghastly hue—but the luminousness of his eye had utterly gone out. The once occasional huskiness of his tone was heard no more; and a tremulous quaver, as if of extreme terror, habitually characterized his utterance. There were times, indeed, when I thought his unceasingly agitated mind was labouring with some oppressive secret, to divulge which he struggled for the necessary courage. At times, again, I was obliged to resolve all into the mere inexplicable vagaries of madness, for I beheld him gazing upon vacancy for long hours, in an attitude of the profoundest attention, as if listening to some imaginary sound. It was no wonder that his condition terrified—that it infected me. I felt creeping upon me, by slow yet certain degrees, the wild influences of his own fantastic yet impressive superstitions.

Column

オスカー・ワイルドが描いた、拒絶された人間にこそある「真実」

自他ともに認める、かっこいい天才

　ヨーロッパには「告白」の文化があります。古くはアウグスティヌスの『告白』から始まり、ルソーの『告白』も有名です。自分の過去を神の前で告白、懺悔するという文学ジャンル。その白眉がオスカー・ワイルドの『獄中記』(De Profundis) です。

　アイルランド生まれのオスカー・ワイルドは、日本でも『サロメ』や『幸福の王子』などの作品で知られ、その耽美的な作風で多くの芸術家たちに影響を及ぼした作家です。

　彼はとにかく若い頃から有名で「私は私の天才以外、申告するものを持ちません」と豪語するほど、才能に恵まれていました。その端麗な容貌と派手な服装、華やかな言動は、常に社交界を賑わせていました。実際、写真を見ても、非常にかっこいいのです。

　ところが、そんな時代の寵児だったワイルドを、一転地獄につき落とすような事件が起こりました。当時のイギリス社会では犯罪と

されていた同性愛の罪で告訴されたのです。彼は投獄され、華々しい社交界の生活から、一気に牢獄でのみじめな生活へと転落しました。プライドは砕け、心はひどく傷つきました。

獄中から「恋人」に宛てた手紙

　獄中から、ワイルドは問題となった「恋人」に向けて手紙を書き送ります。それが、『獄中記』です。人々から褒めそやされる存在から軽蔑される「最低の人間」になって初めて、ワイルドはキリスト教の本質を理解します。この『獄中記』は自己省察の本であると同時に、キリストについてのすぐれた洞察の書でもあります。

　僕がこの作品を読んだのは比較的最近のことです。それまでもワイルドの作品は読んでいましたが、この『獄中記』を読んだときには「やられた！」と思いました。

　聖書の中で、キリストは最も輝かしい存在であるはずなのに、同時に「軽蔑され、拒絶される」存在として登場します。通俗的な慣習になじまず、予定調和的に生きることができない、ある種の天才は「絶対的な魂の孤独者」として社会から排除されるべき運命を背負っている――。ワイルドはそのイメージをキリストに重ねました。社会から軽蔑され、拒絶された人間にこそある「真実」――天才がつかんだ人生の深層は恐ろしく、また美しい世界です。

THE OLD MAN AND THE SEA
by Ernest Hemingway
Copyright© All rights outside U.S., Hemingway Foreign Rights Trust.

J. S. Bach's Goldberg Variation 30 and Aria
CD3に収録したバッハのゴルトベルク変奏曲は、キングレコード株式会社の許可を得て
『J.S.バッハ：ゴールドベルク変奏曲／熊本マリ』(KICC110)より抜粋したものです。

Profile

茂木健一郎(もぎけんいちろう)

脳科学者。ソニーコンピュータサイエンス研究所シニアリサーチャー、慶應義塾大学大学院システムデザイン・マネジメント研究科特別研究教授。1962年、東京生まれ。東京大学理学部、法学部卒業後、東京大学大学院理学系研究科物理学専攻課程修了。理学博士。理化学研究所、ケンブリッジ大学を経て現職。専門は脳科学、認知科学。「クオリア」(感覚の持つ質感)をキーワードとして脳と心の関係を研究するとともに、文芸評論、美術評論にも取り組んでいる。2005年、『脳と仮想』(新潮社)で、第4回小林秀雄賞を受賞。2009年、『今、ここからすべての場所へ』(筑摩書房)で第12回桑原武夫学芸賞を受賞。「CNN English Express」(毎月6日発売、小社刊)にて「茂木健一郎の壁を超える! 英語勉強法」好評連載中。

Staff

デザイン	大下賢一郎
DTP	メディアアート
写真	牧野明神
ルビ訳校閲	Evelyn Corbett
編集協力	石井綾子、三浦愛美、河野美香子、野澤真一
CD朗読	Chris Koprowski、Helen Morrison
CD録音・編集	ELEC(財団法人英語教育協議会)
編集	仁藤輝夫、谷岡美佐子、高野夏奈

モギケンの英語シャワーBOX 実践版
STEP3

2010年11月15日　初版第1刷発行
2013年 5 月 1 日　初版第7刷発行

著者	茂木健一郎
発行者	原　雅久
発行所	株式会社 朝日出版社
	〒101-0065　東京都千代田区西神田3-3-5
	電話　03-3263-3321（代表）
	http://www.asahipress.com
印刷・製本	図書印刷株式会社

ISBN978-4-255-00554-6
乱丁・落丁本はお取り替えいたします。
無断で複写複製することは著作権の侵害になります。
定価は外箱に表示してあります。

©Kenichiro Mogi 2010
Printed in Japan